Contents

THIS month's issue is titled "A Stark Raving Mad Society" and features a painting of Piers Morgan.

I hate Piers Morgan. He represents so much about what's sick about our society. He hosts a Jerry Springer-style program where he regularly brings on people who oppose genocide and people who support it so they can scream at each other and draw clicks and attention with the viral video clips it generates. He morally postures about Gaza when it's convenient while also playing both sides, badgering guests to "condemn Hamas" and shrieking at anti-genocide activists in order to frame himself as a dispassionate neutral observer of a 21st century holocaust. All while comfortably enjoying the fruits of the empire he defends.

All works are written by Caitlin Johnstone and Tim Foley. The Caitlin Johnstone project is 100 percent reader-funded.

Visit caitlinjohnst.one for the original articles and their supporting links.

In This Dystopia

In this dystopia we party downstream from the abuses of the empire like the ravers dancing by the concentration camp on October 7.

We have Jerry Springer-style shows where people who are upset about genocide shout back and forth with people who are enthusiastic about genocide.

We plug our ears into streaming services to drown out the screams and eat snacks to drown out the smell from the black smoke stacks.

We scroll on screens through alternating images of skeletal children and algorithmically boosted celebrity gossip and mutilated bodies and AI art.

We exchange meaningless inanities at social events and fight off the urge to clutch each other tightly and whisper about the terrifying things that are happening to our ecosystem.

We stare at western officials saying peace is preferable but both sides both sides both sides while masturbating furiously behind their podiums.

We stare at pundits saying sure children deserve to eat but Hamas Hamas do you condemn Hamas.

We go to demonstrations and take selfies and hold up signs which say "I oppose this so long as it doesn't disrupt my lifestyle in any meaningful way".

We watch the lights go out in Gaza and watch the light go out in ourselves.

We pray to gods we don't believe in for a future we don't deserve.

We dance by the concentration camp absolutely certain that this is entirely sustainable.

In this dystopia we drift along with the current and ignore the growing roar up ahead. •

Anti-Genocide Activism Is Terrorism In The Empire Of Lies
• Notes From The Edge Of The Narrative Matrix •

British police have been arresting anti-genocide protesters for holding signs expressing support for activist group Palestine Action, which London has now officially designated a terrorist group for putting red paint on war planes that were being used in the Gaza holocaust.

That's right, welcome to the empire, where peace activists are called terrorists, where hospitals are called military bases, where facts are called blood libel, where people opposing genocide are called hateful Nazis, where genocidal soldiers are a protected group and chanting for their death is a hate crime.

•

Israeli outlet Haaretz has published an article titled "Now I Understand Why Israel Is Denying Journalists Access to the Appalling Scene in Gaza" by a French historian named Jean-Pierre Filiu, who spent a month in the killing fields of the ruined Palestinian territory after entering with a busload of French physicians.

Israel has banned journalists from Gaza in order to hide its war crimes, making doctors and other specialists the de facto western reporters on the ground. And they're all reporting the same thing about what they are seeing.

•

Part of the problem is how normies who don't follow this stuff closely cannot believe Israel could be as evil as we're saying it is. They're often like "Oh yeah right, they're just killing civilians because they're evil and want Palestinians to die." Which would make sense as an objection if you hadn't been following Israel's pattern of behavior from day to day and weren't familiar with the way Israelis talk about Palestinians whenever they're speaking to each other in Hebrew instead of addressing the western press.

Israel's public image is somewhat protected by the fact that its behavior is so profoundly evil that simply talking about it strains credulity among the uninformed, in the same way you sound like a crazy conspiracy theorist if you talk about some of the things the CIA has openly admitted to doing in the past. Many people literally cannot believe anyone could be as evil as Israel is, so the true extent of their crimes go unseen.

•

I've decided I'm never going to click on another Piers Morgan Uncensored video. He's just a shitty western empire stooge playing Jerry Springer with people's outrage over the worst things in the world and pretending to be impartial while generating viral online video clips fueled by rage and partisan echo chamber amplification.

It occasionally looks edifying, but it's really a symptom of some of the most diseased aspects of this civilization, like Mr Beast. The man is a parasite feasting on the vitriolic energy of these dark and troubling times, directly profiting from the immense suffering caused by the empire he serves.

•

The western public has stopped viewing Palestine as an intimidating issue to speak out about, and it's causing a major problem for the Israel PR machine.

One of the biggest obstacles for the pro-Palestine movement used to be the way Israel-Palestine was incorrectly regarded as a super complex issue that the average busy member of the public can't hope to understand. That's changing now because a live-streamed genocide is straightforward enough to override the "No you don't understand what's happening because words, words, words" schtick that Israel apologists always use to shut people down, but for a long time the hasbarists were able to intimidate people into silence just by knowing a bunch of clever talking points that the average casual observer would struggle to come up with answers for.

One of my favorite clips from the Glastonbury Festival came from Australian band Amyl and the Sniffers, whose vocalist Amy Taylor gave an off-the-cuff speech about Palestine and colonialism and the parallels between what white colonizers did to Indigenous Australians and what's happening to the Palestinians today.

It wasn't a perfect or super eloquent speech by Taylor's own admission, but it was passionate and it got the point across. At the end she said, "That's the truth and I thought I'd share that today. It was gonna be something way more poetic but that's just what I said; it's not perfect but I think it's better to say anything than to say nothing at all right now."

More and more people are seeing this when it comes to Gaza — that it's better to say anything than to say nothing at all right now. You don't have to be an expert. You don't have to know everything there is to know about about the apartheid state of Israel and the history of the Zionist project. You know what you're seeing and you know it's wrong, and that's enough. Don't let anyone intimidate you into being silent on the defining issue of our times. •

Imperial Hypocrisy About "Terrorism" Hits Its Most Absurd Point Yet

The US has removed Syria's Al Qaeda franchise from its list of designated terrorist organizations just days after the UK added nonviolent activist group Palestine Action to its own list of banned terrorist groups.

The western empire will surely find ways to be even more hypocritical and ridiculous about its "terrorism" designations in the future, but at this point it's hard to imagine how it will manage to do so.

Antiwar's Dave DeCamp writes the following:

> "Secretary of State Marco Rubio announced on Monday that the Trump administration is revoking the Foreign Terrorist Organization (FTO) designation for Hayat Tahrir al-Sham (HTS), the al-Qaeda offshoot that took power in Damascus in December 2024.

> "HTS started as the al-Nusra Front, which was the official al-Qaeda affiliate in Syria until the group's leader, Ahmed al-Sharaa, who is now Syria's de facto president, rebranded. In 2016, Sharaa, who was known at the time as Abu Mohammad al-Jolani, announced he was disassociating from al-Qaeda, and thanked the 'commanders of al-Qaeda for having understood the need to break ties.'

> "Sharaa renamed his group HTS in 2017 and ruled Syria's northwestern Idlib province until he led the offensive that ousted former Syrian President Bashar al-Assad at the end of last year. The US has embraced the new Syrian leader despite his al-Qaeda past, which included fighting against US troops in Iraq."

This move comes as Sharaa holds friendly meetings with US and UK officials and holds normalization talks with Israel, showing that all one has to do to cease being a "terrorist" in the eyes of the empire is to start aligning with the empire's interests.

So that was on Monday. The Saturday prior, the group Palestine Action was added to the UK's list of proscribed terrorist groups under the Terrorism Act of 2000, making involvement with the group as aggressively punishable as involvement with ISIS.

The "terrorism" in question? Spraying red paint on two British war planes in protest against the UK's support for the Gaza holocaust. A minor act of vandalism gets placed in the same category as mass murdering civilians with a car bomb when the vandalism is directed at the imperial war machine in opposition to the empire's genocidal atrocities.

Even expressions of support for Palestine Action are now illegal under British law, leading to numerous arrests over the weekend as activists expressed solidarity with the organization.

Pink Floyd's Roger Waters, who is British, has been formally reported to UK counterterrorism police by UK Lawyers for Israel following the musician's public statement saying "I support Palestine Action. It's a great organisation. They are non-violent. They are absolutely not terrorist in any way."

So let's recap.

Nonviolent protest against a genocide that's being backed by the western empire: Terrorism. Banned. Nobody's allowed to support this.

Being actual, literal Al Qaeda but aligning with the interests of the western empire: Not terrorism. Okie dokie. This is fine.

These hypocrisies and contradictions of the empire are worth drawing attention to because they clearly show that the empire does not stand where it claims to stand. For decades we've been told that western military explosives are falling from the sky in the middle east and Africa because there are terrorists there who need to be stopped, but it turns out "terrorism" is just a meaningless label that means whatever the empire needs it to mean at a given time and place.

Iran's IRGC is labeled a terrorist group because the Iranian military is not aligned with the US empire. Israel's IDF is not labeled a terrorist group despite its constant use of violence upon civilian populations in order to advance political goals. Palestine Action is labeled a terrorist group because it opposes the empire's genocidal atrocities. Al Qaeda in Syria is no longer a terrorist group because it's making nice with Israel and doing what the empire wants.

"Terrorist" just means "anyone who inconveniences the empire in any way." It really is that simple. •

The Empire Is A Nonstop Insult To Our Intelligence

The US has imposed sanctions on UN Human Rights Council Special Rapporteur Francesca Albanese for using her position to oppose the most thoroughly documented genocide in history.

At the same time, the US has removed Syria's Al Qaeda franchise HTS from its list of designated terrorist organizations, because its leader successfully carried out the regime change in Damascus that the western empire had been chasing for years.

At the same time, the UK has added nonviolent anti-genocide activism group Palestine Action to its list of banned terrorist organizations for opposing the Gaza holocaust.

At the same time, the Israeli prime minister who is carrying out that holocaust has nominated the American president who is helping him perpetrate genocidal atrocities for a Nobel Peace Prize.

At the same time, Israel has continued its ban on foreign journalists entering Gaza, while also arresting the Israeli journalist who helped expose the IDF officials who cooked up fake atrocity propaganda about burnt babies on October 7.

At the same time, the Trump administration has enraged its MAGA base by concluding that Jeffrey Epstein had no client list for any kind of sexual blackmail operation and definitely committed suicide.

The western empire is one nonstop insult to our intelligence. The peace advocates are terrorists, the genocide architects deserve peace prizes, the journalists are dangerous, and Epstein was just a wealthy socialite who made a few mistakes.

They do everything they can to make us stupid via propaganda, Silicon Valley information control, and indoctrination schooling systems, and then they treat us like we're morons for the rest of our lives.

The empire depends on ignorance. The more stupid, racist, gullible, and easily distracted we become, the nastier agendas the empire can roll out. Now here we are watching a live-streamed genocide unfold right in front of our eyes for nearly two years while being tube fed a daily diet of the most ridiculous lies imaginable.

As Aaron Bushnell said, this is what our ruling class has decided will be normal. •

Australia Unveils Plan To Fight "Antisemitism" By Crushing Free Speech

As Australia's dear friend Israel announces its plan to move Gaza's entire population into concentration camps to prepare them for deportation and murder them if they refuse, the Australian government is laser-focused on tackling the problem of — you guessed it — antisemitism.

Prime Minister Anthony Albanese made a big spectacle of announcing a new strategy to combat Australia's completely fictional epidemic of "antisemitism" on Thursday, waving around a 20-page plan which is being denounced nationwide as a Trumpian agenda to stomp out free speech in advancement of the interests of the state of Israel.

The author of the plan is Jillian Segal, a career Israel lobbyist born in apartheid South Africa who was named Australia's first Special Envoy to Combat Antisemitism by the Albanese government last year. Segal has had an established record of defending and supporting Israel's genocidal atrocities in Gaza. Her husband John Roth directs one of the major funders of Advance, a climate denying right wing lobbying group which helped kill Australia's Indigenous Voice to Parliament in 2023.

Segal's plan is being slammed as "Trumpian" by free speech advocates because it advocates implementing the US president's policy of cutting off federal funding for universities and other public institutions deemed to be promoting the spread of antisemitism, which of course in effect means protesting against the actions of the Israeli government. Segal writes that she personally "will work with government to enable government funding to be withheld, where possible, from universities, programs or individuals within universities that facilitate, enable or fail to act against antisemitism."

Segal calls for all public institutions to be forced into espousing the International Holocaust Remembrance Alliance's (IHRA) working definition of antisemitism, which has been opposed around the world for its conflation of criticism of Israel with hateful actions toward Jews. Under the IHRA definition it is considered antisemitic to claim that Israel is a racist endeavor, or to compare Israel's abuses to those of Nazi Germany — both of which are entirely legitimate criticisms which should be put forward far more often than they are.

Here is a summary of the full scope of Segal's plan written up by the ABC's Tom Crowley:

Education — a greater role for the Envoy to resource and educate the community, schools, businesses and public institutions about antisemitism and to embed an understanding of antisemitism in law enforcement, government agencies and the school curriculum.

Universities — call to withhold public funding to universities or those within them deemed to "facilitate, enable or fail to act" on antisemitism, and an inquiry into "clusters" of antisemitism if encampments continue into 2026.

Media — a new role for the Envoy to encourage media organisations to "avoid accepting false or distorted narratives" and encourage public broadcasters to "accurately and positively" represent Jewish history and culture and make programs that support "social cohesion".

Arts — a recommendation that there be protocols for arts festivals and organisations to respond to antisemitic incidents, with public funding able to be withheld similar to universities.

Policing — a permanent standing arrangement for law enforcement agencies to co-operate on investigating antisemitism, similar to the Avalite taskforce set up after the Adass synagogue attack.

Online hate — stronger regulation of online hate speech and algorithms, and the ability to support "trusted voices" to refute antisemitism on social media, plus a review of hate speech laws.

Migration — screen visa applicants for antisemitism and ensure the Migration Act effectively facilitates visa cancellations for antisemitism.

As you can see, Segal is demanding the authority to exert control over pretty much every major aspect of Australian society. She is claiming she wants to do this to combat antisemitism, but everyone knows she actually wants to do this to promote the interests of Israel, because that's what these things always mean in practice.

Segal's plan claims that "manipulated narratives in the legacy media" are driving antisemitism and accuses the Australian press of "misinformation", asserting that "publicly funded media organisations should be required to uphold clear editorial standards that promote fair, responsible reporting to avoid perpetuating incorrect or distorted narratives or representations of Jews."

Segal says that under her plan she will "monitor media organisations to encourage accurate, fair and responsible reporting and assist them to meet their editorial standards and commitment to impartiality and balance and to avoid accepting false or distorted narratives."

Asked on the ABC on Thursday to list some of the changes that she would make to the reporting of public news broadcasters, Segal adamantly refused to give a single example, despite being repeatedly pressed to do so by the ABC's Sarah Ferguson.

The following morning Segal was interviewed on the ABC's Radio National Breakfast and pressed on the same issue, where she finally relented and gave one single example of absolutely breathtaking ridiculousness.

"Six months ago or so," Segal said, "the ABC ran a story repeatedly about a hospital in Gaza that had been bombed. And there was incomplete information, as there is only perhaps information emanating from Hamas, but it was alleged to be, the ABC reported as fact, that it had been bombed by Israel. And then horrified people were upset and the Jewish community was looked at with disgust and worse. And then it turned out indeed that it was not bombed by Israel, that it had been from Gaza itself, and it had been a bomb that had fallen short."

Segal appears to be referring to one of the early bombings of the al-Ahli Arab Baptist Hospital, which occurred not six months ago but in October of 2023. Israel and various western institutions claimed the hospital was accidentally bombed by Palestinian forces while analysts like Forensic Architecture say the attack came from Israeli forces, accusing Israel of peddling misinformation about the strike. Since that time Israel has deliberately demolished Gaza's health infrastructure with hundreds of attacks on healthcare facilities, and the al-Ahli Hospital has been bombed no fewer than eight separate times.

Segal's one and only example is a perfect illustration of the kind of extreme bias she wants to impose upon Australian consciousness, which obviously has no place in a free society.

The fraudulent antisemitism panic in Australia has been reinvigorated by two events last week that were seized upon with shrieking hysteria by the mainstream press, none of which showed any signs of an antisemitism crisis in our nation.

As Paul Gregoire explains for the Sydney Criminal Lawyers blog, Australia is being whipped up into a frenzy by the conflation of one incident in which a Sydney man set fire to the doors of a Melbourne synagogue with a different and completely legitimate act of anti-genocide activism.

The synagogue attacker is yet another story of a shady individual with no known record of antisemitic ideology or pro-Palestinian sentiment perpetrating an apparent antisemitic attack, following a long stretch of supposed antisemitic incidents which turned out to have been staged by organized crime operatives with no ideological motive.

This one dubious story of a man committing an actual crime against an actual Jewish place of worship has been obnoxiously mentioned in the same breath as another unconnected incident by the entire Australian political/media class all week. Protesters gathered at the

Miznon restaurant in Melbourne to demonstrate against the establishment's Israeli co-owner, who is also the spokesperson for the so-called Gaza Humanitarian Foundation where Israeli soldiers admit they've been massacring starving civilians seeking food. A fight broke out with a group from the restaurant across from Miznon who the protesters say instigated the attack and who are clearly seen assaulting the pro-Palestinian activists in the available video footage.

The entire so-called "antisemitism crisis" in Australia is like this. The overwhelming majority of it is just people criticizing Israel and trying to do what they can to stop the live-streamed genocide they've been watching on their screens every day for two years, which is then deliberately conflated with the actions of a few fringe actors with frequently suspicious motives.

"Antisemitism" means criticism of Israel. That's just what it means now. It used to mean something else, but years of bad faith actors using that word in the most dishonest ways imaginable to defend the most horrific things you've ever seen has changed the definition. It is no longer possible to separate that word from this sustained campaign of mass deception.

It's the genocide. People are mad at the genocide. They don't hate Jews, they hate genocide. This was explained quite nicely the other day by Jack Mirkinson, who wrote the following about the controversy surrounding musical duo Bob Vylan's chants of "Death to the IDF" at Glastonbury Festival last month:

"Left unmentioned in any of this freakout is the context in which it is taking place. Why was Bob Vylan talking about Palestine right now? Why was a giant crowd of people so receptive to these comments? Why has this become such a totemic issue?

"The answer will not shock you. It's because Israel has been committing genocide in Gaza for nearly two years.

"That's it! That's why. People don't like genocide, and when they see a country committing genocide, they stop liking that country so much. If the genocide ended, a lot of people would be less mad at Israel than they are right now.

"This isn't rocket science. But — and this is the crucial thing — because our world's leading politicians and media outlets fundamentally don't see opposition to the genocide as a legitimate viewpoint to hold, they can't quite comprehend what is happening all around them."

That's it. It's the genocide, stupid. That's all this has ever been about. I wish I could force every pundit, politician and journalist in Australia to listen to these words. •

The Good Guys

The Good Guys are building concentration camps in Rafah
and massacring civilians trying to obtain food.

The Good Guys are circling the planet with hundreds of military bases
and telling us we're not allowed to oppose genocide.

Yesterday I saw a little girl playing
and I thought how nice it is that she has all her limbs
and that she is not lying still
covered in gray dust
while her father screams and cries
and calls out to God
while trying to kiss her back to life.

The world is changed now.
The moon is covered with powdered buildings.
The pigeons are weeping
and the wind sounds like drones.
Sometimes I cough and gray dust comes out.
Sometimes it's a child's shoe.
There's a dead donkey lying in my backyard
that nobody wants to talk about.

The Australians chat about real estate investments
and how you can knock down one house
and replace it with two houses
and then make believe that neither house
smells like corpses.

The news man tells us the corporations
are just dumping the products directly into the Pacific now
while clinging tightly to the edge of the screen
so the black hole doesn't pull him in.

Everything's fine, the news man yells,
and the system is working perfectly.
We are the Good Guys after all.
We are, after all, the Good Guys.

.

Genocide Summer Camp, And Other Notes From The Edge Of The Narrative Matrix

It really is nuts how a young person can fly to Israel and go play genocide games in Gaza for a while and then just fly back to their own country and expect to be treated like a normal member of society like it's some kind of genocide summer camp.

•

The narrative about an "antisemitism crisis" in our society has two main components:

1. Redefining "antisemitism" to mean "criticism of Israel", and

2. Pretending not to see a connection between rising incidents of "antisemitism" as it's been redefined and Israel perpetrating an active genocide.

•

"Antisemitism" means criticism of Israel. That's just what it means now. It used to mean something else, but years of bad faith actors using that word in the most dishonest ways imaginable to defend the most horrific things you've ever seen has changed the definition.

It is no longer possible to separate that word from this sustained campaign of mass deception. You can only have governments, institutions and individuals use a word differently for so long with such a high degree of uniformity before the definition changes.

Word definitions change over time depending on how people use them. Nice used to mean stupid. Explode used to mean applaud. The word meat used to refer to any kind of food, not just animal flesh. The meanings changed because enough people started using them to refer to something else, in exactly the same way we've seen occur with the word antisemitism.

That's locked in. It has already happened. Everyone knows that antisemitism refers to criticism of Israel and its actions and antisemite refers to someone who does so. Everyone understands this regardless of whether they support Israel or oppose it. That is the definition now.

If you want a word for someone who thinks Hitler was correct or uses triple brackets and posts big nose memes online, you're going to have to make up a new word, because antisemite is taken. You can't even really use "Jew hater" either, because that meaning is being polluted in the exact same way antisemite has been. You have to make up an entirely new word, and use it consistently.

Israel's spinmeisters will deny this publicly, even though they know it's true. They'll say it's possible to criticize Israel without being an antisemite, but if you ask them to name someone who regularly and forcefully criticizes Israel's genocidal atrocities in Gaza whom they don't consider antisemitic, they won't be able to. Every single person who criticizes Israel with appropriate consistency and force is branded an antisemite (or perhaps "self-hating" if they happen to be Jewish), without a single, solitary exception.

These aren't my rules, they're the rules of the Israel apologists. I'm just pointing out the obvious fact that those rules have been set.

•

A new report from WIRED has found that the supposedly "raw" video footage of Jeffrey Epstein's prison cell which Trump's Department of Justice released to prove Epstein committed suicide was in fact digitally manipulated.

"Metadata embedded in the video and analyzed by WIRED and independent video forensics experts shows that rather than being a direct export from the prison's surveillance system, the footage was modified, likely using the professional editing tool Adobe Premiere Pro," the report reads. "The file appears to have been assembled from at least two source clips, saved multiple times, exported, and then uploaded to the DOJ's website, where it was presented as 'raw' footage."

This just keeps getting better and better.

Epstein is officially a leftist conspiracy theory now. Rightists dropped it when they supported the president who's covering it up, so now it's ours. From now on if you want to talk about Epstein you are joining the side of the commies. Welcome to the revolution, comrade.

•

The Australian government is imposing age verification laws for internet use which may require digital IDs from people of all ages who want to use major online platforms, at the same time this same government is pushing to stomp out and censor all criticism of Israel.

Doesn't take a genius to see where this is going. •

Don't Take Instruction On How To Live Your Life From A Stark Raving Mad Society

Don't take instruction on how to live your life from a stark raving mad society.

This civilization is sick. It is genocidal. It is ecocidal. It is omnicidal. We are ruled by psychopaths, while the best among us are relegated to the fringes of the fringe. We are hurtling into totalitarianism and armageddon at breakneck pace while our attention is aggressively pulled toward the vapid and the inane.

You should share none of the values and priorities of this freak show. You should not let any aspect of this dystopia inform your decisions regarding who you should be and what kind of life you should live.

In this warped and twisted madhouse, we are trained to believe that "success" looks like making a lot of money, earning large amounts of esteem and adoration, having a certain body type, living in the right kind of neighborhood in the right kind of house full of the right kind of products to impress the right kind of people. We are trained to believe we need to rack up all kinds of accomplishments, academic achievements, promotions, impressive stories, social ascendence. We are trained to believe we must attract a certain type of partner who will be approved of by everyone whose approval we crave.

If we cannot achieve these goals, we are trained to believe we should feel bad about ourselves. That we don't deserve happiness. That we should either spend our time stressing and striving for worthiness as defined by our crazy civilization, or go and join the ocean of miserable failures who couldn't win the capitalism game and sedate ourselves with alcohol and entertainment waiting for death to carry us into the nothingness where we belong.

This is clearly insane. It's a stupid game with stupid prizes. The only reason anyone takes it seriously is because we were raised and taught how to live by other people who take it seriously. Our parents have been indoctrinated into the power-serving worldview that has been forcibly imposed upon the denizens of the empire, and we want to make them proud. Our friends, families and acquaintances have been likewise brainwashed, and we want to impress them.

But to do so is to take lessons on how to live from a collective disease that is pointed at misery and dysfunction. It is impossible to lead a truly fulfilling life while also trying to live the way the people around us think we should live, because the society which shaped their ideas about how we should live is insane.

If you want to really live an awake and inspired life, you've got to blaze your own trail. You've got to unlearn everything you've been told about what a life properly lived would look like, and write your own rules. Because the rules everyone else has been playing by were written by madmen.

Find your own truth. Set your own values and priorities. Define your own idea of success. Define your own idea of sanity. Consider the possibility that just being present for the beauty of each moment on this wonderful planet is worth more than anything the imperial insane asylum has to offer you. Consider the possibility that your very next breath, deeply relished, would be enough.

We are destroying our planet and driving every living organism toward annihilation. The status quo has failed as spectacularly as anything could possibly fail. The old ways of doing things plainly do not work. So try some new ways.

Be different. Be strange. Be a freak. Do everything the wrong way. Disappoint your parents. Fail to live up to your potential. Transgress your family doctrine. Anger whatever gods you were taught to believe in. Nothing anyone has done has worked. It is therefore necessary to travel off the beaten path.

The world won't get better until humanity changes its ways. Humanity won't change its ways if it keeps insisting on trying the same failed approaches over and over again. Our survival as a species depends on diverging from our patterns.

Maybe we'll succeed in surviving, and maybe we won't. But at the very least we can rescue ourselves from spending one more day on this amazing blue world trying to live by the rules of lunatics. •

The New York Times Finally Stops Avoiding The G–Word

The New York Times has published an op-ed by a genocide scholar who says that he resisted acknowledging the truth of what Israel is doing in Gaza for as long as he could, but can no longer deny the obvious.

It's an admission that may as well have come from The New York Times itself.

In an article titled "I'm a Genocide Scholar. I Know It When I See It.", a Brown University professor of Holocaust and genocide studies named Omer Bartov argues that "Israel is literally trying to wipe out Palestinian existence in Gaza," and denounces his fellow Holocaust scholars for failing to acknowledge reality.

"My inescapable conclusion has become that Israel is committing genocide against the Palestinian people," Bartov writes. "Having grown up in a Zionist home, lived the first half of my life in Israel, served in the I.D.F. as a soldier and officer and spent most of my career researching and writing on war crimes and the Holocaust, this was a painful conclusion to reach, and one that I resisted as long as I could. But I have been teaching classes on genocide for a quarter of a century. I can recognize one when I see one."

And resist he did. In November 2023,

Bartov wrote another op-ed for The New York Times saying "As a historian of genocide, I believe that there is no proof that genocide is currently taking place in Gaza, although it is very likely that war crimes, and even crimes against humanity, are happening."

Apparently he is seeing the proof now and has stopped resisting what's been clear from the very beginning. And it would seem the editors of the Gray Lady have ceased resisting as well.

The New York Times, which has an extensively documented pro-Israel bias, has frenetically avoided the use of the g-word on its pages from the very beginning of the Gaza onslaught. Even in its opinion and analysis pieces the NYT Overton window has cut off at framing the issue as a complex matter of rigorous debate, with headlines like "Accused of Genocide, Israelis See Reversal of Reality. Palestinians See Justice." and "The Bitter Fight Over the Meaning of 'Genocide'" representing the closest thing to the pro-Palestinian side of the debate you'd see. During the same time we've seen headlines like "From the Embers of an Old Genocide, a New One May Be Emerging" used in reference to Sudan.

In an internal memo obtained by The Intercept last year, New York Times reporters were explicitly told to avoid the use of the word "genocide", as well as terms like "ethnic cleansing" and "occupied territory".

"'Genocide' has a specific definition in international law," the memo reads. "In our own voice, we should generally use it only in the context of those legal parameters. We should also set a high bar for allowing others to use it as an accusation, whether in quotations or not, unless they are making a substantive argument based on the legal definition."

Earlier this year the American Friends Service Committee cancelled its paid advertisement in The New York Times calling for an end to the genocide in Gaza, saying the outlet had wanted them to change the word "genocide" to "war" in order for their ad to be published.

So there has been a significant change.

To be clear, this analysis by Omer Bartov is not significant in and of itself. He is only joining the chorus of what has already been said by human rights organizations like Amnesty International, Human Rights Watch, United Nations human rights experts, and the overwhelming majority of leading authorities on the subject of genocide.

What is significant is that even experts who've been resisting acknowledging the reality of the genocide in Gaza because of their bias toward Israel have stopped doing so, and that even the imperial media outlets most fiendishly devoted to running propaganda cover for that genocide have run out of room to hide.

The Israel apologists have lost the argument. They might not know it yet, but they have. Public sentiment has turned irreversibly against them as people's eyes are opened to the truth of what's happening in Gaza, and more and more propagandists are choosing to rescue what's left of their tattered credibility instead of going down with the sinking ship.

Truth is slowly beginning to get a word in edgewise.

Keep pushing. Keep fighting. Keep resisting.

It's working. •

Trump Has Completely Dropped His "Populist" Act

It's so funny how Trump has stopped even pretending to be a populist. As soon as he was re-elected he was just "Yeah okay so Israel comes first and forget everything I said about free speech and the Ukraine war is continuing and there will be no Epstein investigation, fuck you."

It has long been obvious to anyone with half a brain that Donald Trump is just another Republican swamp monster playing on public discontent with the status quo to win votes and support, but it is genuinely surprising how completely he has stopped pretending to care about fighting the deep state and sticking up for ordinary Americans as soon as he got back into office. He's just dropped the populist schtick entirely and is giving the finger to anyone who complains.

The president has been aggressively and repeatedly demanding that his entire base shut up about Jeffrey Epstein and move on after years of MAGAworld fixation on the story, bizarrely going as far as claiming that interest and attention on the Epstein files was a concoction of the Democrats. He is doing this even as his Department of Justice releases a video which it claims disproves conspiracy theories that the sexual predator was murdered in his prison cell — but the video is edited and missing minutes of footage.

This happens as the Financial Times reports that Trump is now encouraging Ukrainian president Volodymyr Zelensky to ramp up deep strikes into Russian territory and asking whether it would be possible to hit Moscow. This would be the same President Trump who falsely promised on the campaign trail that he would end the Ukraine war in "no longer than one day."

After pledging to restore and protect free speech in the United States, Trump has been aggressively stomping out speech that is critical of the state of Israel and its genocidal atrocities, scoring yet another win for government censorship on Tuesday with Columbia University's announcement that it is adopting the IHRA definition of "antisemitism" which conflates criticism of Israel with hate speech against Jews, in accordance with the wishes of the Trump administration.

After promising to "restore peace, stability, and harmony all throughout the world," Trump has bombed Iran, poured weapons into Israel and Ukraine, backed Israel's genocide in Gaza and its numerous acts of war against its neighbors, slaughtered hundreds of civilians with a savage bombing campaign in Yemen, and conducted dozens of airstrikes in renewed operations in Somalia, all while leading the nation into the era of official trillion-dollar Pentagon budgets.

In 2023 Trump proclaimed that "if you put me back in the White House... I will totally obliterate the deep state." In 2025 he's advancing pretty much every longstanding deep state agenda in the book.

Every single part of Trump's platform where he could have claimed to be standing up for the little guy against the powerful has been completely flushed down the toilet in the first six months of his second term, leaving only a standard George W Bush Republican in its place. If you wanted tax cuts for the rich and cruel treatment for immigrants then Trump is still your man, but if you were hoping he'd benefit ordinary Americans or do anything to drain the swamp in Washington he's just peeing on you and writing a wall of text on Truth Social explaining why the pee is actually rain.

Which again should come as no surprise to anyone who's been paying attention. No real change will ever come from either of America's two power-serving major parties.

But what's so funny is people are probably just going to fall for it again. Trump's base is very upset about the Epstein thing and many of them might actually abandon Trump himself, but you know next election cycle someone like Tucker Carlson or JD Vance will run on his platform and these suckers will swallow it hook, line and sinker. I actually said this on Twitter the other day and got multiple people telling me that actually Tucker Carlson getting elected would be a major blow to the deep state, so you know they're already primed for it. They can't wait to fall in line behind the next phony Republican populism scam.

Whatever. People will be fed whatever slop they keep asking for. The lesson will keep on repeating until it is learned. •

•

If You're Still Supporting Israel In 2025, There's Something Wrong With You As A Person

Sometimes I think it's astonishing how aggressively Israel's supporters work to stomp out criticism of Israel. Then I remember that these people also support mass murdering children; trying to take away my speech rights is one of their less evil goals. It shouldn't shock me.

I saw someone talking online about how crazy it is that music groups who speak out against Israel's atrocities are starting to form alliances with each other in an effort to counteract the campaign to silence them and destroy their careers, saying it shouldn't be necessary to form an alliance in order to oppose an ongoing genocide. And that's true, it shouldn't be necessary. But it also shouldn't surprise us that people who think bombing hospitals is fine would try to cancel musicians for criticizing Israel.

One mistake westerners keep making is thinking of Israel's supporters as normal people with normal moral standards just because we happen to know them and interact with them in our communities. They look like us, speak like us, dress like us and act like us, so we assume they must think and feel a lot like us as well.

But they don't. If you're still supporting Israel in the year 2025, there's something seriously wrong with you as a person. You do not have a normal, healthy sense of empathy and morality.

It's 2025. Israeli soldiers are telling the Israeli press that they're being ordered to massacre starving civilians trying to obtain food from aid centers. Countless doctors have been telling the world that Israeli snipers are routinely, deliberately shooting children in the head and chest throughout the Gaza Strip. Amnesty International, Human Rights Watch, and all the leading genocide experts and human rights authorities are saying that a genocide is being perpetrated in Gaza. The New York fucking Times just published an op-ed by a Zionist genocide scholar who's finally admitting that it's a genocide.

There's no way to deny what this is anymore. If you still support Israel in the year 2025, it's not because you don't believe Israel is committing horrific atrocities. It's because you believe those horrific atrocities are good, and you want to see more of them.

Most Israel supporters will deny that this is the case, because they lie. They lie constantly. They have no moral problem with lying. They have no moral problem with burning children alive, so of course they have no problem with lying.

That's where people go wrong. They assume Israel supporters can't possibly be lying about their concerns about "antisemitism" in order to promote the information interests of Israel, because nobody could be that evil. But Israel supporters think it's fine to intentionally starve babies by blockading baby formula from entering Gaza. Of course they are that evil.

People assume Israel's supporters wouldn't deliberately stage fake antisemitic incidents or artificially inflate antisemitism figures in their own countries so that their governments will implement authoritarian measures to stomp out criticism of Israel in the name of fighting antisemitism, because they assume nobody could be that depraved. But these people think it's fine for the IDF to systematically assassinate Palestinian journalists to stop them from telling the truth. Of course they are that depraved.

Of course they'd try to silence our speech. Of course they'd try to send our kids off to war with Iran. Of course they'd work to manipulate our government. Of course they'd pollute the information ecosystem with mountains of lies. They support a live-streamed genocide. They're bad people.

Supporting Israel and its actions is not some political opinion like your position on property taxes or marijuana legalization. It's not just some people having a point of view we need to respect and treat as equal to our own view on the matter. They're working to make it possible to conduct an extermination campaign

of unfathomable horror. That's as political as a gang rape, and just as worthy of respect.

There's not really anything you can put past Israel's supporters at this point. They will lie. They will manipulate. They will pretend to believe things they do not believe. They will pretend to feel things they do not feel. And they will do these things to facilitate some of the worst atrocities you can possibly imagine.

This is who Israel's supporters are. They're showing you who they are every single day. •

AOC Is A Genocidal Con Artist

The Democratic Party's Instagram-friendly progressive darling Alexandria Ocasio-Cortez has voted with the overwhelming majority of House representatives against withholding $500 million in missile funding for Israel, despite previously saying that Israel is committing "a genocide of Palestinians" in Gaza with US support.

The only lawmakers voting to withhold the military aid were Democrats Ilhan Omar, Rashida Tlaib, Summer Lee and Al Green, and Republicans Thomas Massie and Marjorie Taylor Greene.

Coming under fire from the left for the glaring contradiction of providing military assistance to a state that is perpetrating an active genocide, AOC issued a statement claiming her vote was about protecting civilians.

The statement reads as follows:

"Marjorie Taylor Greene's amendment does nothing to cut off offensive aid to Israel nor end the flow of US munitions being used in Gaza. Of course I voted against it.

"What it does do is cut off defensive Iron Dome capacities while allowing the actual bombs killing Palestinians to continue.

"I have long stated that I do not believe that adding to the death count of innocent victims to this war is constructive to its end. That is a simple and clear difference of opinion that has long been established.

"I remain focused on cutting the flow of US munitions that are being used to perpetuate the genocide in Gaza."

AOC's statement is absolute crap. The Iron Dome is not used for defending, it's used to facilitate constant attacks.

In an article for Jewish Currents titled "Iron Dome Is Not a Defensive System," Dylan Saba explains:

"By almost entirely negating the ability of militant groups in Gaza to respond to Israel's incursions, the purportedly defensive Iron Dome allows Israel to strike without fear of repercussion. And because the cost is so low when measured in Israeli casualties, Israel can wage perpetual war without suffering domestic political consequences, and is under negligible pressure to pursue diplomacy with the Palestinians. 'In theory, a weapon like Iron Dome could be used only defensively. But in practice it doesn't work that way,' analyst Nathan Thrall told Jewish Currents. 'Iron Dome facilitates greater Israeli offensive measures, because it lowers the perceived cost to Israel of escalating or extending or initiating attacks.' In other words, while the Iron Dome may prevent the deaths of Israeli non-combatants, it has made it easier for Israel to engage in deadly operations that take Palestinian lives."

The Iron Dome isn't for protecting civilians, it's for protecting the Israeli regime from deterrence. We see this in the comfort the regime displays in waging constant military violence on its neighbors knowing they can't retaliate. That's why Israel cut a ceasefire deal with Iran so fast.

Iran's advanced missiles can't be reliably stopped by the Iron Dome, so Iran was able to smash Israel and force it to cease its unprovoked aggressions. If Israel had had a missile defense system which could casually swat those missiles out of the sky at a high rate of success, Israel would still be bombing Iran today, and would continue doing so until Tehran looked like Gaza. Israel's war-horny population would have supported this, because they'd have no skin in the game.

Saying you support funding Israel's "defensive weapons" while opposing sending it "offensive weapons" is as nonsensical as saying you would never give a mass shooter guns and ammunition, but you would give him body armor to keep him safe from the police. You're helping him commit mass murder just as much as you would be if you gave him guns and ammo. Kings didn't arm their knights with shields and armor so that they

could live long and fulfilling lives, they did it so the knights would live long enough to kill the people the kings wanted killed.

If you believe a state is committing genocide, there is no justifiable reason for you to support enhancing that state's military capabilities and helping it defend itself from those who try to stop it. As others have pointed out, this is exactly the same as opposing Hitler's Holocaust but supporting giving anti-aircraft flak cannons to Nazi Germany.

It's a self-evidently ridiculous, warmongering, and ultimately genocidal position, disguised as progressive humanitarianism. It's all the ugliest things about western liberals.

People who say you should criticize AOC less because there are way worse members of congress act like she's just passively sitting there being a mediocre lawmaker. She's not. She's actively anchoring the leftmost edge of the Overton window of US politics to militarism, capitalism, colonialism, and genocide. She's actively stopping American politics from moving any further left than the nightmare we see before us.

Leftists shouldn't hate AOC less than the politicians to her right, they should hate her much more. It isn't Mike Johnson's responsibility to move the US government to the left, and it's not Nancy Pelosi's job. It's hers. That's what she was elected to do. That's what she framed the

goals of her entire political career as being. And she's taking her stand firmly bracing against any leftward movement from America's genocidal, warmongering, unjust, exploitative, tyrannical status quo.

And that's what she was actually put there to do. Her real job is to say "thus far and no further" to the leftmost end of the political spectrum of the world's most powerful and destructive government. That's the Democratic Party's job in general, and it's the job of media-savvy progressive Democrats in particular. They are there to provide as little resistance as possible when US politics are shoved toward more genocidal, militaristic, oligarchic, capitalist, imperialist abuses, and to provide as much inertia as possible to any movement in the opposite direction.

That's why people who seek leftward movement in the US political machine see AOC as one of their main enemies. It's for the exact same reason you'd see someone actively blocking the fire exit as your enemy when trying to escape from a burning building. •

Israel's Depravity Will Always Find New Ways To Shock You

• Notes From The Edge Of The Narrative Matrix •

A doctor in Gaza named Nick Maynard reports that Israeli snipers are now shooting starving civilians in different body parts on different days, based on the injuries people show up with for treatment. There's a head day, a leg day, a genitals day, etc.

"The medical teams here have also been seeing a clear pattern of people being shot in certain body parts on different days, such as the head, legs or genitals, which seems to indicate deliberate targeting," Maynard says.

I keep thinking there's nothing Israel could do that would shock me anymore, but they keep finding ways.

•

The Israeli military has attacked the residence of World Health Organization staff, detaining multiple medical workers. This comes as Israel's Trade Envoy Fleur Hassan-Nahoum tells Channel 4 News that "most doctors in most hospitals in Gaza" are "involved in terrorist activities".

Possibly the single dumbest thing Israel and its apologists ask us to believe is that Israel has been systematically demolishing Gaza's healthcare infrastructure because the healthcare infrastructure is full of terrorists, and not because they want to commit genocide.

•

The Gaza Health Ministry announced on Monday that among the 130 Palestinians killed in the daily death toll of Israel's genocidal onslaught, 99 were killed while trying to obtain food from aid sites.

At some point you just run out of words for talking about how evil this shit is.

•

If you want to find out who someone truly is, surrender fully to their will and give them everything they want. They'll show you.

Zionism is showing us what it truly is right now. This is what it looks like when the Zionists are allowed to do exactly what they want to do.

•

Hasbarists have been going nuts on social media lately. Whenever Israel is acting more evil than usual the online Israel apologia always kicks into high gear.

Words words words words words words words. They love their words. They think if they say enough words with enough feigned conviction people will go "Oh okay well maybe starving civilians to death is actually fine and normal after all."

•

I'll never get used to the way I'm watching my own government and its allies support the most nightmarish shit I've ever seen in my life every single day in the middle east and yet people keep trying to convince me to be really fearful and hateful toward Muslims.

•

Alexandria Ocasio-Cortez has been having a public tantrum on Bluesky because of the leftist backlash from her vote against an amendment which would have blocked funding for Israel's missile defense system and her garbage justification of that move, angrily proclaiming that her "record on Palestine speaks for itself" and claiming that the opposition has created a "threat environment" that is "scary".

That AOC chose to throw this fit on Bluesky rather than Twitter is telling; she got so mad that she ran to the liberal echo chamber where she's adored in order to complain about how the left won't even let her support just a little bit of genocide as a treat.

This is just her yelling at people for not loving her when she does gross

swamp monster things. But it doesn't work that way. You don't get to be the beloved leftist people's champion and also be the person who votes against an amendment to withhold $500 million of military funding for a genocidal state and then justifies it with obnoxious lies. You don't get to do the darling of the left thing and also do the weird Zionist swamp creature thing. You have to pick one, because you can't be both. No amount of yelling at ordinary people is going to change that.

AOC and her supporters wouldn't have to spend days frantically justifying her refusal to support Palestine and oppose genocide at every opportunity if she would simply support Palestine and oppose genocide at every opportunity. That's normal. Just be normal. Do the normal thing. •

Gaza Isn't Starving, It Is Being Starved

Malnutrition-related deaths in Gaza are beginning to climb, with the health ministry reporting 18 in a single 24-hour period. Doctors report that people are "collapsing" in the street, and Gaza journalist Nahed Hajjaj is warning the world not to be surprised if the remaining reporters in the enclave are soon silenced by starvation.

Unless something drastically changes, things can be expected to get much worse very rapidly.

Meanwhile Israeli forces are setting new records with their massacres of starving civilians seeking aid, with 85 killed in a single day on Sunday.

If this isn't evil, then nothing is evil. If Israel isn't evil, then nothing is.

So what's the plan here? Do we just sit and watch Israel starve Gaza to death with the support of our own governments?

And then what? We just go along with our lives, knowing that that happened? That this is what we are as a society? That our civilization is comfortable allowing something like that to happen? And that our rulers could do the same thing to another inconvenient population at any time?

We're just meant to be cool with that? And go on living like it's normal?

I'm genuinely curious. How exactly is everyone planning to go about living their lives after that point? How does that work, exactly?

I'm asking because I don't know. I mean, I know what my own government and its allies should do, but I don't know what we as ordinary members of the public are supposed to do.

You'll see western pundits and politicians asking "How do we get a ceasefire in Gaza?" or "How do we end hunger in Gaza?" as though it's some kind of ineffable mystery, which is kind of like a man strangling a child to death while saying "The child is being strangled, but HOW do we stop the child strangulation from occurring?"

It's not some mystery how to get a ceasefire in Gaza; the empire is the fire. It simply needs to cease firing. Israel's holocaust in Gaza is made possible only by the support of its western backers, primarily the United States. Numerous Israeli military insiders have acknowledged that none of this would be possible without US support. If the United States and its western allies ceased backing Israel's onslaught in Gaza, a ceasefire would have to occur.

Likewise, it is not a mystery how to get food into Gaza. You just drive the food on in and give it to people.

They've got roads and gates right there. The only reason people in Gaza are starving is because western governments (including my own Australia) conspired to pretend to believe that UNRWA is a terrorist organization to justify cutting off critical aid, while doing nothing to pressure Israel into allowing aid to flow freely.

And now Israel and the US empire are monopolizing the delivery of "aid" through the so-called Gaza Humanitarian Foundation, whose facilities now see civilians massacred every day for the crime of attempting to obtain food.

The organizations, funding and delivery systems to feed Gaza are all 100 percent fully available (at no cost to Israel, by the way). They're just not being allowed to provide aid because the goal is to remove all Palestinians from Gaza via death or displacement. The people of Gaza are starving because the west is helping Israel starve Gaza. It really is that simple.

This isn't some kind of unfortunate famine caused by a drought or natural disaster. It is a deliberately manufactured starvation campaign, implemented with genocidal intent.

To paraphrase Utah Phillips, Gaza isn't starving, it is being starved. And the people who are starving it have names and addresses. •

It's A Genocide, But It's Also So Much More Than That

The mass atrocity in Gaza is a genocide, obviously, and is an undisguised ethnic cleansing operation.

But it's also a lot more than that.

It's an experiment — to see what kinds of abuses the public will accept without causing significant disruption to the imperial status quo.

It's a psychological operation — to push out the boundaries of what's normal and acceptable in our minds so that we will consent to even more horrific abuses in the future.

It's a symptom — of Zionism, of colonialism, of militarism, of capitalism, of western supremacism, of empire-building, of propaganda, of ignorance, of apathy, of delusion, of ego.

It's a manifestation — of violent racist, supremacist and xenophobic belief systems that have always been there but were previously restrained, meeting with the unwholesome nature of alliances that have long been in place but have been aggressively normalized.

It's a mirror — showing us accurately and impartially who we currently are as a civilization.

It's a disclosure — showing us what the western empire we live under really is underneath its fake plastic mask of liberal democracy and righteous humanitarianism.

It's a revelation — showing us who among us really stands for truth and justice and who has been deceiving us about themselves and their motives this entire time.

It's a catalyst — a galvanizing force and a rallying cry for all who realize that the murderous power structures we live under can no longer be allowed to stand, and a blaring alarm clock opening more and more snoozing eyes to the need for revolutionary change.

It's a test — of who we are as a species and what we are made of, and of whether we can transcend the destructive patterning that is driving humanity to its doom.

It's a question — asking us what kind of world we want to live in going forward, and what kind of people we want to be.

It's an invitation — to become something better than what we are now. •

Know Them By Their Fruits

They're doing it right in front of us. Right in front of us.

So many people have dedicated their entire lives working to expose the criminality of the empire, and then the empire comes right out and commits a live-streamed genocide right in front of us.

Whistleblowers. Investigative journalists. Authors. Documentarians. Conspiracy analysts. Peace activists. Their whole lives devoted to the task of uncovering the crimes of the undeclared empire we live under and drawing attention to them, saying "Look! See?? We really are ruled by monsters!" Only for the monsters to come right out and intentionally starve children to death on all our screens all around the world.

People like me are almost redundant at this current point in history. I've been writing about the depravity of the empire for years, thousands of articles and millions of words, and I've never said anything that illuminates the reality of our situation nearly as well as the fact that western governments and media have openly colluded with Israel to exterminate a group of innocent people because they're the wrong ethnicity.

I mean, what could I possibly say about that that they're not already saying themselves? The message is already there, fully baked. Perfect. Complete. They're telling us everything we could possibly need to know. There's nothing I could add.

I don't have much use for scripture, but if I had to pick a favorite line from the Bible it would be "You will know them by their fruits." Those seven little words cut through all the lies and distortions of life under the western empire, because they tell us to stop paying attention to all the spin and PR and justification and excuses we hear from the imperial propaganda machine, and just look at the products of the empire on their own. Ignore their words, and watch the results of their actions.

Those tiny skeletal bodies you're seeing on your social media feed are the fruits of the empire. The shredded, eviscerated, decapitated children you've been seeing in footage from Gaza since 2023 are the fruits of the empire. This is known now, and it can never be unknown.

As Maya Angelou said, "When someone shows you who they are, believe them the first time. People know themselves much better than you do. That's why it's important to stop expecting them to be something other than who they are."

This is who they are. This is who our leaders are. This is who our complicit news media are. This is what Israel is. This is what Zionism is. This is what the empire is. This is what western civilization is. We know that now. We know them by their fruits.

This is who they are, and it's who they'll always be. That's why it's important never to forget what they've shown us about themselves in Gaza, and to never, ever forgive them.

Our rulers have shown us that they must not be allowed to rule any longer. The empire has shown us that it should not be allowed to dominate our planet any longer. The apartheid state of Israel has shown us that it should not be allowed to exist any longer. Western supremacism, Zionism, racism and imperialism have shown us that these things must be eradicated from our world.

They have planted seeds of knowledge inside you about who they are and the status quo we're being asked to consent to. Let those seeds sprout and grow. Tend to them with care. Help them to flourish.

Someday the tree that they planted in us will bear fruit of its own. •

They're Starving Civilians To Steal A Palestinian Territory, And They're Lying About It

Just so we're all absolutely clear about what we're watching here, Israel is intentionally starving civilians in order to bring about the ethnic cleansing of Gaza and steal a Palestinian territory. That's all this is, and anyone who says otherwise is lying.

This isn't a theory. This is what's happening. The facts are in and the case is closed. Israeli officials aren't even hiding it anymore.

Israel's Heritage Minister Amichai Eliyahu is telling the Israeli media that "the government is racing ahead for Gaza to be wiped out," and that "all Gaza will be Jewish."

Israel's National Security Minister Itamar Ben-Gvir is tweeting in Hebrew that a "complete halt of 'humanitarian aid'" will allow "encouragement of migration" and "settlement" in the Gaza Strip.

Israeli Defense Minister Israel Katz announced earlier this month that the official plan is to build a giant concentration camp for Gaza's population on the ruins of Rafah while working to deport the population to other countries.

Prime Minister Benjamin Netanyahu himself made it clear back in May that implementing Donald Trump's plan for the ethnic cleansing of Gaza was a precondition to having peace in the enclave.

Trump made it clear back in February that his plan was for "all" Palestinians to be removed from the Gaza Strip on a "permanent" basis.

Within days of Israel's assault on Gaza in October 2023, Israel's Intelligence Ministry was circulating a plan for the entire population of Gaza to be moved to the Sinai Peninsula in Egypt, and an Israeli think tank had drawn up a strategy for the "relocation and final settlement of the entire Gaza population."

Indeed, Israel has been on record scheming to find a way to relocate the population of Gaza for many decades.

That's what this is all about. That's all this has ever been about. It's not about hostages. It's not about Hamas. It's not about Israel defending itself. It's about stealing a Palestinian territory, and anyone who says otherwise is lying.

And the lies have been erupting like a geyser in recent days. Israel and its apologists have been frantically pushing the narrative that Gaza is starving because the UN isn't allowing aid in (swiftly refuted by Drop Site News), that Gaza is starving because Hamas is stealing the aid (swiftly refuted by Reuters), and that Gaza is starving because Hamas attacks people who try to go to aid sites (already refuted by Israeli soldiers telling the Israeli press that they're the ones shooting the aid seekers).

The more evil Israel gets, the more frenetic its apologists need to get with their lies to justify its behavior.

Starvation deaths in Gaza are skyrocketing. Many of those still alive have already suffered permanent damage, and even with a massive influx of aid and complete reversal of Israeli policies it will be very difficult to undo the effects of the famine.

Western governments are beginning to speak out against the mass atrocity in Gaza, far too little and far too late. We can expect Israel and the United States to respond to this outcry by saying that Palestinians need to be evacuated out of Gaza as quickly as possible in order to rescue them from this deliberately manufactured humanitarian crisis. We can expect them to denounce anyone who opposes this ethnic cleansing operation as evil monsters who want to starve the poor Palestinians.

And it will all be lies. They lied this entire time.

It's about the most evil thing you could possibly come up with, really. If this is not evil, then nothing is. •

They Intend To Keep Lying About Gaza Until They've Emptied It Out
• Notes From The Edge Of The Narrative Matrix •

We're back at the part of the news cycle where Israel tells the world it's going to allow a bit more aid into Gaza in order to mollify its allies and reduce the public outcry as images of starving children draw objections from the west.

This is just Israel giving the Kier Starmers and Anthony Albaneses of the western world just enough of an excuse to go silent about the starvation of Gaza again. They will then continue starving Gaza. This psychopathic python-like suffocation tactic is how Israel has gotten Gaza to the point it's at now.

And of course it's worth noting that Israel's announcement that it will allow more food into Gaza so people don't starve completely debunks all its claims these last few days that people in Gaza are starving because of Hamas and the UN. They're starving because Israel is starving them.

•

Israeli officials have told The New York Times that there has never been any evidence of Hamas stealing aid from UN trucks in any significant way, a claim Israel and its apologists have been falsely asserting for two years. They lie about everything. They never stop lying.

We've been asked to believe a lot of intensely stupid narratives throughout this genocide, but "it's actually HAMAS who's starving Gaza" has got to be the dumbest one yet. The fact that Israel and its supporters tried to blame the UN and Hamas for Israel's extensively documented starvation campaign makes it clear that these freaks intend to keep lying about this thing until the last dying gasp of the last Palestinian.

•

Gideon Levy has a new article out titled "Denying Gaza's Starvation Is No Less Vile Than Denying the Holocaust". Personally I'd take it much further and say it's vastly worse than denying the Holocaust, because it's helping to kill people right this very moment.

•

I'm sorry if this is antisemitic but I think it's wrong to deliberately starve thousands of children to death.

·

If you found out someone was trapping small children in a confined space and then intentionally starving them to death, what words would you use to describe that person?

Think about how fucked up you'd need to be inside to starve a baby, or to support someone who is doing so. Think how many millennia of evolutionary conditioning you'd have to override as a human, as a primate, as a mammal, to stifle the screaming you feel inside when you see a skeletal infant. You'd have to make yourself less of a human inside to support the inhumanity.

·

The worst thing Donald Trump has ever done is commit genocide in Gaza. Everything else pales in comparison. He could end the Gaza holocaust with a phone call just like Biden could have, and he hasn't. For that reason alone he deserves to die in a cage.

·

Children's Youtube star Ms Rachel has announced that she won't be working with anyone who doesn't publicly oppose Israel's genocide in Gaza.

The thing I love about Ms Rachel is that nobody was pushing her to speak out about Gaza. Not one person was out here saying "Ms Rachel's silence on Rafah is deafening!" She could've gotten away with being silent on Gaza forever and suffered no professional consequences, but she spoke out anyway because she's a genuinely good person.

·

Today I got my first comment telling me I was wrong to oppose Israel in October 2023 but now I'm right because things have changed. I expect to receive many more such comments going forward as people navigate the difficult cognitive dissonance terrain of realizing they've been wrong this entire time.

·

Israel apologists love using circular reasoning to dismiss outlets and organizations which criticize Israel. If you've ever argued with them online you know what I'm talking about.

It's basically this —

Normal person: Here's evidence of Israel doing bad things.

Israel apologist: You can't cite THAT outlet! That outlet is Hamas propaganda!

Normal person: What? What makes them Hamas propaganda?

Israel apologist: They're always saying Israel does bad things!

Or this —

Normal person: Israel is committing genocide.

Israel apologist: Nuh-uh, that's blood libel.

Normal person: Amnesty International, Human Rights Watch and UN human rights experts all say it's genocide.

Israel apologist: Those groups are antisemitic!

Normal person: What? Why do you say that?

Israel apologist: They're always spreading antisemitic lies about Israel!

Normal person: Such as?

Israel apologist: Such as saying Israel is committing genocide!

•

Everyone spreading lies today to help Israel carry out the final stages of its final solution knows exactly what they're doing. We see you, you sick fucks. We'll remember you forever. •

It Shouldn't Have Taken This Much For Mainstream Voices To Start Speaking Up About Gaza

Israel's top human rights group B'Tselem has finally declared that Israel is committing genocide, as has the Israel-based Physicians for Human Rights. The Israeli organizations join Amnesty International, Human Rights Watch, UN human rights experts, and the overwhelming majority of leading authorities on the subject of genocide in their conclusion.

The debate is over. The Israel apologists lost. And we are seeing this reflected in mainstream discourse.

Pop megastar Ariana Grande has started speaking out in support of Gaza, telling her social media followers that "starving people to death is a red line." This is a new threshold. Opposing Israel's genocide is now the most mainstream as it has ever been.

MSNBC just ran a piece explicitly titled "Israel is starving Gaza. And the U.S. is complicit.", featuring a segment with the virulently pro-Israel Morning Joe slamming the mass atrocity. CNN's Wolf Blitzer, himself a former AIPAC employee, has done a 180 and is now raking Israel over the coals on the air for its deliberately engineered starvation campaign. The New York Times finally overcame its phobia of the g-word with an op-ed titled "I'm

a Genocide Scholar. I Know It When I See It."

We're now seeing notoriously Zionist swamp monsters in the Democratic Party like Barack Obama, Hakeem Jeffries, Cory Booker and Amy Klobuchar changing their tune and attacking Netanyahu and Trump for their joint genocide project in Gaza, with increasingly forceful pushback from some on the right like Marjorie Taylor Greene as well.

Zoom image will be displayed

As western pundits, politicians and celebrities suddenly pivot to denouncing Israel's genocidal atrocities after two years of silence, it's hard to believe that just a few weeks ago we were being told that saying "death to the IDF" is a hate crime.

People who've been staring at this genocide from the beginning have been asking the entire time, what is it going to take? What will it take for our society to stop sleepwalking through inane trivialities and vapid distractions and start opposing the holocaust of our day?

Raining military explosives on a giant concentration camp packed full of children wasn't enough.

Burning children alive wasn't enough.

Systematically destroying Gaza's entire healthcare infrastructure — up to and including entering hospitals they've attacked and destroying individual pieces of medical equipment one by one — wasn't enough.

Killing more journalists than were killed in both World Wars plus the US Civil War, the Korean War, the Vietnam War, the Yugoslav Wars, the War in Afghanistan, and the ongoing war in Ukraine wasn't enough.

The systemic rape and torture of prisoners wasn't enough.

IDF soldiers routinely sharing photos and videos of themselves mockingly dressing in the clothes of dead and displaced Palestinian women and playing with the toys of dead and displaced Palestinian children wasn't enough.

Israeli officials openly expressing genocidal intent for the people of Gaza wasn't enough.

The US president and Israeli prime minister openly declaring their goal of the complete ethnic cleansing of a Palestinian territory wasn't enough.

Field testing new weapons of war on Palestinians like they're guinea pigs in a laboratory wasn't enough.

Leaving countless civilians to slowly suffocate or die of dehydration trapped under the rubble of bombed buildings wasn't enough.

Creating an AI system to ensure that suspected Hamas fighters are bombed when they're at home with their children and naming it "Where's Daddy?" wasn't enough.

Using Palestinians as human shields wasn't enough.

Burying injured civilians alive with bulldozers wasn't enough.

The IDF admitting to running a popular Telegram channel called "72 Virgins" which posted extremely gory and sadistic snuff films of people in Gaza being butchered by Israeli forces wasn't enough.

IDF snipers routinely shooting children in the head and chest throughout the Gaza Strip wasn't enough.

The IDF flying drones which play the sounds of crying babies at night in order to lure out hiding civilians to murder them wasn't enough.

IDF troops telling the Israeli press that they're being ordered to massacre starving civilians seeking food from aid sites wasn't enough.

Israeli snipers targeting different body parts of starving civilians on designated days — leg day, head day, genitals day, etc — wasn't enough.

Far right Israeli citizens setting up blockades to stop aid trucks from entering Gaza while they enjoyed parties and barbecues at the blockade sites wasn't enough.

Using lies and propaganda to dismantle the aid system for bringing essential food and life-supporting supplies into Gaza, to replace it with a US/Israeli op where aid seekers are massacred every single day, wasn't enough.

Using siege warfare to deliberately starve Gaza for the previous 22 months wasn't enough.

But now that starvation has hit a critical point and deaths from malnutrition are skyrocketing, now that images of dead skeletal children are filling our screens, now that the damage to organs and brains from starvation will be irreversible in many cases — now it's enough.

That was the line, apparently. That's what mainstream western consciousness has decided is too much. Everything up until that line was fine, but now it's not fine anymore.

And the killing is still going on. The sudden awakening of conscience hasn't translated into any material actions or changes at all yet. If it had come in October or November 2023 like it should have we might be seeing that opposition translate into actually saving Gaza by now, but the light has only just been switched on. It's not even guaranteed that those who are speaking up will continue to do so.

I'm glad people are waking up to the cruel reality of this nightmare. I'm grateful to each and every influential voice who uses their platform to speak out, even at this late date. I truly am.

But I also think we need to take a very hard, very uncomfortable look at ourselves as a society right now. If all those monstrous abuses were tolerable for us over these last two years, there's something deeply and profoundly sick about our civilization.

We are not living right. We are not thinking right. We are not feeling right. We are warped and twisted. The information we consume and the norms we've been conditioned to accept have corrupted our souls.

We have been made into something bad. Something ugly. Something shameful. Something we need to do everything in our power to change.

We need to rescue ourselves from what we have become. We need to transform, deeply and radically, into something that could never again allow something like this to occur.

The way things are clearly isn't working. The mainstream worldview is clearly a lie. Everything we've been taught to believe about our society, our nation, our government and our world was clearly false.

We need to fight our way through the cognitive dissonance of recognizing that our entire way of looking at things as a collective has failed, and we need to find a new way of being.

Otherwise we're going to keep being smashed in the face with increasingly horrifying reminders of what we have allowed ourselves to become.

The lessons will repeat until they are learned.

We had better start learning them. •

Israel Apologists Support Genocide; Of Course They're Fine With Lying

Israel apologists use language the same way malignant narcissists do. It's never to communicate or connect or find out what's true, it's always to manipulate and get things they want.

Not one person sincerely believes Israel isn't starving Gaza. Everyone knows it is, including the people who are saying it isn't. They're just throwing a bunch of language at it in an effort to keep the west supporting Israel's genocide.

Israel's official Twitter account is currently trying to claim that a photo of a dead skeletal man proves people are sharing disinformation about Israel, because it turns out the man had diabetes. Back in December 2023, Human Rights Watch published an article titled "Gaza Blockade Puts People with Diabetes at Risk." It's a well-documented fact that the first people to die in a famine are always small children and people with health problems, and yet the main hasbara arguments today are "Why is it always the children dying and not the healthy adults?" and "This person already had health problems!"

Just this morning I had someone on Twitter show me pictures which they claimed proves Gaza is not currently starving, and the pictures were from the West Bank.

Before that another hasbarist responded to footage I shared of far right Israelis blocking aid trucks into Gaza saying, "the trucks have been stopped because they are full of weapons heading to Hamas." When I called him out for lying he said "why not? you all take AI produced photos and videos and run on the narrative that they are real." Neither of these statements are true. He knew he was lying, and he didn't care.

These are just some things I saw this morning before coffee.

They do this all the time. They lie and lie and lie and lie and lie. They are not normal people. They do not use language the same way normal people do.

Which should come as no surprise to anyone. If you'd support a genocide, of course you'd be willing to lie in order to justify it. If your moral line isn't drawn before genocide, of course it's not going to be drawn before lying either.

Zoom image will be displayed

Another, more heartening, thing I saw on Twitter today was Israel apologists talking to each other about how their PR is failing and the media aren't helping them.

"Israel needs a PR Iron Dome. It's a matter of national security," tweeted one.

"Our Hasbara isn't working," responded another. "We sit in a bubble of confirmation bias preaching to each other about things we know already. We're not spreading the truth and we're not coming up with any solutions to it. We really suck at this and we're being too stupid to see our way out of it."

"I have been saying they need a new army unit dedicated to just this (and combatting misinformation and disinformation)," said someone else.

In a separate conversation I saw another hasbarist admonishing his peers to "stop saying Israel is doing bad PR" and calling on Jewish billionaires to start paying influencers to promote Israeli information interests.

I find all this both encouraging and hilarious. They're losing control of the narrative, and they know it.

My favorite is the "we need a PR Iron Dome" one, because what could that possibly look like that Israel doesn't already have? Lobby groups? Think tanks? Paid influencers? Online shills? A wildly sympathetic and some would say sycophantic mainstream press? How much more narrative control could Israel and its supporters possibly have?

And how revealing is it that simply ending the genocide never at any time enters the conversation? The world hates Israel because Israel is committing genocide, but they never see that as the problem — they see bad PR about the genocide as the problem. The problem isn't that we're doing genocide, the problem is that we're not using the right words to explain why the genocide is good.

Again, these are not normal people. There's got to be something seriously wrong with you as a person to keep supporting Israel in the year 2025. •

In The Age Of AI, We Each Have To Choose How Much Of Our Humanity We Want To Keep

Elon Musk's AI chatbot Grok has gone full Nazi after changes were made to its programming to give it a heavier right wing bias, sparking international headlines with its tweets praising Adolf Hitler's treatment of Jews and babbling about Jewish conspiracies to spread anti-white hate.

The official X account for Grok announced that the team is "aware of recent posts made by Grok and are actively working to remove the inappropriate posts," saying "xAI has taken action to ban hate speech before Grok posts on X."

So apparently they're having a hard time teaching their chatbot specifically what kind of right wing bias they want it to have.

Shit's getting weird, man. The age of AI is weird.

AI is presenting a very interesting dilemma to each of us. We now each have to decide as individuals just how human we wish to keep our experience, because we're hitting a point where we can become just about as divorced from the things that make us human as we want to be.

We can choose to let AI do our critical thinking for us if we want to. We can choose to let it do our reading and writing for us. We can choose to let it create the art we produce and consume. We can choose to let it formulate arguments for us justifying our opinions and our worldview, or to let it reshape our worldview altogether. We can even choose to anthropomorphize it and have relationships with it if we are lonely.

We all have to choose for ourselves where the line is now. What point we will not cross beyond. What parts of our humanity we are willing and unwilling to trade for convenience or cognitive ease.

Just how far into the guts and gristle of humanity do you want to be?

How deeply do you want to be immersed in the breathing, sweating, pulsing fleshiness of the human adventure?

How fully do you want to feel the erotic ticklings of creativity moving through you, and the frustration you'll experience on the days when it doesn't show up?

To what extent do you want to experience the highs and lows of intimate human relationships, and all the unpredictability and insecurity that comes with them?

How much cognitive discomfort are you willing to push through in order to form a new opinion, learn about a new subject, or understand an unfamiliar idea?

How separated are you ready to become from that within us which produces the perfectly imperfect art, music and literature of our species?

How much do you want to feel the earth beneath your feet, the wind in your hair, and the sacred thrum of existence in your veins?

These didn't used to be questions we needed to answer for ourselves. If we wanted something written, we had to write it. If we didn't know how to write, we had to learn. If we didn't put in the work, the thing we wanted to write never got written.

Now it's a conscious choice for us how far we're each willing to move into this new AI thing. We all have to decide for ourselves how far is too far, with the understanding that every step we take in that direction is costing us something. Maybe something very dear to us. Maybe something we can never get back. •

Those Who Were Wrong About Gaza Should Admit It With Profound Humility

A liberal Israel apologist named Brianna Wu has made a mealy-mouthed tweet acknowledging the reality of what's happening in Gaza that is so obnoxious I need to have a quick rant about it.

Wu, who has managed to translate her public attention from the 2014 Gamergate harassment scandal into a role as a pro-Israel spinmeister, tweeted a screenshot from a New York Times headline titled "Total Failure': Israel's Return to War Heaped Ruin on Gaza and Did Little for Israelis", captioning it as follows:

> This was A1, above the fold in the Times today.
>
> I support Israel as strongly as someone can, and I have extreme concerns about their past reporting. But every other paper is saying the same thing, so I have to conclude that finally, after countless exaggeration, the cries of wolf are actually true.
>
> Israel has every right to defend itself and it has every right to exist. But I didn't check my brain or my conscience at the door. Many friends who've stood with Israel all along share my concerns.

This enrages me in ways I'm struggling to fully articulate.

"After countless exaggeration, the cries of wolf are actually true"? So it wasn't exaggeration or crying wolf then was it, you fucking asshole? Almost like you've spent two years defending A FUCKING GENOCIDE and attacking anyone who opposed it?

This whole post reads like it was rewritten a dozen times, carefully pared down until it was stripped of all meaning and said almost nothing. She's admitting that she was wrong, but it's just kind of dribbling out of the corner of her mouth as she sidles out the door while giving us all the finger.

This is the same person who wrote in The Boston Globe that "my fellow leftists are betraying our Jewish allies" and claiming "the casual antisemitism I'd looked past in progressive spaces became impossible to ignore" because the left was opposing the mass atrocity she now acknowledges we are seeing in Gaza. The same person who falsely claimed that "Civilians have never been targeted in Gaza" and that the onslaught "has the lowest civilian to combatant deaths in the history of modern urban warfare". Who earlier this very month was complaining about "how susceptible we are to the 'genocide' propaganda" about Gaza.

I mean, how is she not weeping for mercy on her knees right now? How is she voicing these side-mouthed "concerns" while still accusing the people who've been speaking out about this of "crying wolf", instead of desperately begging the people of Gaza for forgiveness?

If I had just realized I had helped butcher people by the tens of thousands, I personally do not think I could go on living. Like, I actually don't think my organs would keep functioning. I can't even imagine that I'd want them to.

Brianna, do you know what you have done? Have you fully taken account of your part in the horrific pain and unfathomable suffering that you have facilitated over the past 22 months?

Because you are not just some rando on the internet who didn't do her due diligence. Your words ran cover for a genocide. You are as guilty as Goebbels. You orchestrated PR campaigns with people whose publicly stated intention was to ethnically cleanse the Gaza Strip of Palestinians. They were saying it with their mouth holes as far back as October 2023, and every time they did you doubled down.

This is not something you can just brush off, either legally or morally.

Legally you are as culpable as Julius Streicher who hanged for his offenses in World War II.

Morally, if you fully humbled yourself to the horrors you had enabled, you would've fallen to the floor, praying for forgiveness for every child whose legs were ripped from their little bodies by shrapnel, who roam the tent cities orphaned and alone, who died of thirst trapped in a rubble tomb crying for their mother who lay dead just feet away from them. There are literally tens of thousands of stories just like this, and you carry blame for every single one of them.

Do you understand that? You can't. I don't believe it. If you did, every cell of your body would be trying to jump away from itself in the pure crystalline revulsion of that realization. If you fully took account and responsibility for your part in this man-made catastrophe you wouldn't need to be hanged — the depth of your own shame for your actions would be too much for your body, and you would collapse internally. Your heart would stop out of sheer shock.

The other day I wrote, "Today I got my first comment telling me I was wrong to oppose Israel in October 2023 but now I'm right because things have changed. I expect to receive many more such comments going forward as people navigate the difficult cognitive dissonance terrain of realizing they've been wrong this entire time."

We're seeing more and more of this as the truth emerges. I read another tweet by Yahoo Finance's Jordan Weissmann saying, "As Dems converge on agreement that Israel has been committing an atrocity, I do think there needs to be some reckoning among mods that, while lots of ugly antisemitism burst from the left after Oct. 7, the leftists were fundamentally more right about what this war would become."

"Ugly antisemitism", Jordan? That "antisemitism" was people opposing the atrocities you now admit we were right about. If you're going to admit you were wrong, just do it. Don't try to drag down those of us who've been correct the entire time while you right your own wrongs.

This can't be how people acknowledge they were wrong about Gaza as the truth comes out and becomes undeniable. It can't be. This cannot stand. People absolutely should admit that they were wrong, and they absolutely should be encouraged to do so, but they need to do it with humility, and with some outward expression of remorse. Because they just spent two years of their lives promoting some of the very worst things that could possibly happen on this earth.

Try again, Brianna. Try to muster up some sincerity this time. •

Israel Apologists Think "No No, We're Starving SICK Kids!" Is A Winning Argument

*I will probably spend the foreseeable future periodically reminding the world that when everyone was angry at Israel for starving children in Gaza, Israel's apologists spent days loudly proclaiming that no, they were actually just starving **sick** children.*

As their **defense** they said this. They actually believed this helped their case.

Let me back up a bit.

On Wednesday, The New York Times posted an editor's note on an article it had published the previous Friday which included a horrifying photo of an emaciated child named Mohammed Zakaria al-Mutawaq. Caving to pressure from Zionists and influence ops like the Israeli propaganda outlet HonestReporting, the Times went out of its way to clarify that al-Mutawaq "had pre-existing health problems," which Israel apologists instantly and predictably spun as proof that the media are lying about Israel starving Gaza.

Former Israeli prime minister Naftali Bennet claimed that The New York Times was guilty of "a blood libel in 2025."

Israeli media outlets like The Times of Israel, The Jerusalem Post, i24 News, YNET and Israel Hayom went ballistic, as did Jewish News Syndicate.

"New York Times stunningly rolls back claims about viral photo of starving Gaza boy," reads a New York Post headline.

"New York Times admits using misleading cover photo of emaciated Gaza child," blared Fox News.

"NYT Adds Sick Editors' Note to Viral Photo of Child Starving in Gaza," proclaimed The New Republic.

Conservative pundit Glenn Beck threw a furious shit fit.

AIPAC hilariously accused the notoriously pro-Israel New York Times of being "instinctively against Israel".

Israel apologists like David Frum, Gad Saad, Brianna Wu, Eyal Yakoby, Eylon Levy, Batya Ungar-Sargon, Eli David, Stephen L Miller, David Collier, Noah Pollak, and John Podhoretz went nuts on Twitter.

"They quietly added an editor's note, but the lie already went global," tweeted the Israel Foreign Ministry account.

Zionist billionaire Bill Ackman said that Israel should sue The New York Times and other outlets for libel.

CNN's Scott Jennings tweeted that the photo was evidence that a "propaganda mission" had been fulfilled.

And it was all complete bullshit. All of it.

Any expert in the field will tell you that the first people likely to die in any famine will be young children, the elderly, and people with chronic health problems. Mohammed Zakaria al-Mutawaq is two of the three. Israel apologists are citing obvious evidence that Gaza is being starved and claiming it's evidence that Gaza is not being starved, and bizarrely acting as though sick children being starved to death makes Israel look better instead of worse.

An independent fact-checking platform called Misbar reports the following:

"Misbar interviewed Hedaya al-Mutawaq, the mother of 19-month-old Mohammed Zakaria al-Mutawaq, and found Israeli claims about her son's condition to be misleading.

"'My son Mohammed was born in December 2023, during the war, without any chronic illnesses,' Hedaya told Misbar. 'Doctors diagnosed him with macrocephaly, which they said was caused by nutritional deficiencies during pregnancy due to the Israeli war.'

"She emphasized that Mohammed was healthy and of normal weight at birth. 'Over the past four months of displacement, his condition worsened due to the severe shortage of food. That is when he developed acute malnutrition.'

Misbar included a photo of Mohammed which his mother provided, showing a healthy-looking infant prior to Israel's increased starvation campaign.

So Israel is killing disabled kids using siege warfare to deprive them of food and medical care, and its defenders are claiming this makes Israel look like the heroes in this story rather than the villains. It takes a special kind of psychopathy to think this is a winning argument.

This isn't even the only time they've done this.

The other day Israel's official Twitter account tried to claim that a photo of a dead skeletal man proves people are sharing disinformation about Israel, because it turns out the man had untreated diabetes. Back in December 2023, Human Rights Watch published an article titled "Gaza Blockade Puts People with Diabetes at Risk."

Israel's COGAT account tweeted that "Hamas is using photos of sick children to push the 'starvation' narrative and blame Israel" by pointing out that a starving 14 year-old child in a photograph actually has "a genetic disease."

They're actually trying to argue that people with chronic illness suffering under a siege more than healthy people is evidence of their innocence, rather than the normal thing you'd expect to be seeing at this point if Israel was intentionally starving a civilian population.

This is a new level of disgusting, in two years of record-shattering levels of disgusting.

I don't expect that I will ever let Israel's supporters live this one down, and neither should you. •

Marjorie Taylor Greene Called It A Genocide Before Bernie Sanders
• Notes From The Edge Of The Narrative Matrix •

MAGA wingnut Marjorie Taylor Greene is calling the Gaza holocaust a genocide while progressive hero Bernie Sanders continues to adamantly refuse to do so, despite the solidified consensus among human rights groups and genocide experts that that's what this is.

This is humiliating for everything that passes for the "left" in mainstream US politics. Imagine being such a dogshit human being that you'd let Marjorie Taylor Greene be a better person than you.

I keep seeing people say we shouldn't use the label genocide until Israel has been found guilty by an international court, but that's exactly the same as saying you can't say a murderer is trying to murder someone and intervene to stop him until he has been convicted of murder in a court of law.

•

France, the UK and Canada are saying that they intend to recognize a Palestinian state in September. It's unclear what this would look like, how it would happen, or how it would address any of the Israeli atrocities we're witnessing at the moment.

I mean, the US and Israel are openly and explicitly saying they're going to empty all the Palestinians out of Gaza. What are they going to do, stick a Palestinian flag in the empty field of rubble? If they were serious about stopping this nightmare they'd be talking about hard economic sanctions.

•

Those who say everything Israel is doing in Gaza can be explained by October 7 have got it exactly backwards: everything we're seeing in Gaza explains why October 7 happened in the first place.

The sadism and psychopathy we're witnessing in Gaza didn't magically appear 22 months ago; everyone in Gaza has been experiencing Israel's abusiveness in various manifestations throughout their entire lives. Israel has always been this way. October 7 just gave it the excuse to completely unleash its genocidal impulses.

•

People still supporting this genocide really think they'll be able to use "I didn't know Israel was lying" to defend themselves when this all comes crashing down.

You fucking knew. You knew the whole time. You lied your way into this, but you won't be able to lie your way out.

•

Israel's strongest propaganda weapons are western governments, the western press, legions of paid trolls, and an extremely powerful lobby.

Palestine's strongest propaganda weapons are Israel's actions, raw video footage, facts, journalism, and the "translate from Hebrew" button.

•

Gosh I wonder what else the Palestinians have been right about the entire fucking time?

•

Israel and its supporters constantly frame Israel's actions as representative of all Jews everywhere. They'll deny it, but it's true. That is indisputably what you are communicating when you accuse everyone who criticizes Israel's actions of hating Jews.

Israel is doing the worst things anyone has ever seen under a Star of David banner and claiming to represent all Jews when they do it. Where do people expect this to lead? Do they think it will lead good places?

The truth is that Israel and its supporters have done more to promote hatred of Jews in the last 22 months than all the neo-Nazis and antisemitic conspiracy theorists on earth have in the last eighty years. Nobody is fomenting hatred of Jews more rapidly and effectively than the genocidal apartheid state which claims to represent all Jews.

•

Everyone complains that Israel and its apologists lie constantly, but, I mean, of course they're going to lie. Have you seen what the truth looks like?

•

Hating Israel without also hating the US-centralized western power structure that backs it is a silly and nonsensical position.

•

Historically, those who commit genocide have always had stated justifications for their actions. They've always claimed they were defending themselves. They've always denied they were in the wrong. They didn't twist their mustaches like cartoon supervillains cackling about how fun it is to do genocide and be evil, they provided reasons and explanations for why what they were doing was right.

The fact that Israel has arguments and apologia defending its actions doesn't negate the conclusively established fact that Israel is committing genocide. Of course they're justifying their actions and claiming they're in the right; that's what always happens.

•

I'm having trouble finding the words to talk about the people who are scurrying around lying and manipulating to excuse the deliberate starvation of civilians in Gaza today. "Evil" doesn't cut it. "Monster" and "psychopath" are too kind.

How do these people live with themselves? They have to live each and every moment of their lives inside the sort of brain that would produce this kind of behavior. I sincerely cannot imagine living life in that way, for even one day.

Israel supporters are so shockingly, venomously evil that it makes you stop and re-evaluate everything you think you know about humanity. Every spiritual, philosophical and psychological insight you've arrived at over the course of your life will struggle to make sense of the freakish, gratuitous sadism you'll witness in Israel's apologists describing their own thoughts in their own words. It actually makes you question your entire worldview.

I'm out of words. I write words for a living, and I have no words. There is nothing I can say. •

"What Was Israel Supposed To Do After October 7?" Is Asking The Wrong Question

As Israel and its supporters continue to lose control of the narrative around the world with more and more people awakening to the reality that a genocide is taking place in Gaza, I'm seeing the resurrection of a talking point that western Israel apologists have been trying to make work off and on since this mass atrocity began.

"What was Israel supposed to do in response to October 7?" they ask confidently, taking it as a given that there is no possible answer to this brilliant checkmate question besides "Rain vast quantities of military explosives on a giant concentration camp full of children and deliberately starve a civilian population using siege warfare."

But the real problem is that they are asking the wrong question.

A much more useful and interesting question than "What was Israel supposed to do in response to October 7?" is "What were Palestinians supposed to do in response to all of Israel's abuses prior to October 7?"

Nobody's ever been able to give me a serious response to this question which doesn't entail mountains of lies and/or the dehumanizing expectation that Palestinians should accept conditions that none of us would willingly accept ourselves.

That's why you never see me criticizing Hamas. If someone could tell me what specifically Palestinians should have done in response to Israel's tyranny that they haven't already tried in order to obtain real material justice, I'd happily say Hamas should have taken that option instead of resorting to violent force. But if that option truly existed, Hamas never would have been created in the first place. That's why nobody's been able to tell me what such an option would have looked like without lying.

What was Israel supposed to do after October 7? Same thing they should have done before October 7: dismantle the apartheid state, give everyone equal rights, pay massive reparations, and right all the wrongs of the past. October 7 was a response to the tyranny and abuse of Israel; the correct thing to do when things finally came to a head with the Hamas attack would have been to remove all the tyranny and abuse which gave rise to it.

That's what Israel should have done. Of course Israel was never going to do this, for the same reason they spent decade after decade murdering, displacing and oppressing Palestinians since Israel was created. Israel would never allow justice and equality after October 7 for the same reason Israel would never allow justice and equality before October 7: because Israel has always been a settler-colonialist project that can only be sustained by nonstop violence and tyranny and theft and abuse and lies and breathtaking immorality.

That is the reason October 7 happened, and it's the problem all decent people in the world are trying to address right now.

Those who suggest that everything Israel is doing in Gaza can be explained by October 7 have got it exactly backwards: everything we're seeing in Gaza explains why October 7 happened in the first place.

The sadism and psychopathy we're witnessing in Gaza didn't magically appear 22 months ago; everyone in Gaza has been experiencing Israel's abusiveness in various manifestations throughout their entire lives.

Israel has always been this way. October 7 just gave it the excuse to completely unleash its genocidal impulses. •

Israel's Genocidal Intentions Have Been Obvious This Whole Time

Liberal Israelis are slowly beginning to join the rest of the world in admitting that what's happening in Gaza is a genocide — a fact that has been clear to anyone with eyes and a basic sense of morality from the very beginning of this nightmare.

It was obvious in October 2023 that Israel intended to eliminate all Palestinians in Gaza, in part because you would never treat a population that way if you intended to leave survivors on your border. Because you'd know they'd seek revenge later on.

Call it the Inigo Montoya problem — if you kill someone's father right in front of him, it's a safe bet that he's going to spend the rest of his life trying to kill you. If you intend to act in monstrous ways that fill young children with thoughts of revenge, then you need to get rid of the children, and you need to get rid of the women who will give birth to them. Otherwise you're just creating a problem for your own children and grandchildren down the road.

The Nazis understood this. Heinrich Himmler famously said, "I did not feel I had a right to exterminate the men — i.e. kill them or have them killed — while allowing the children to grow up and take revenge upon our sons and grandsons. We had to reach the difficult decision of making this nation vanish from the face of the earth."

The savagery of Israel's post-October 7 onslaught was so horrific right off the bat that it was clear they didn't intend to leave anyone alive in Gaza. It was clear they intended to kill as many people as possible and force any survivors to leave, because there's no way they'd be acting with such sadistic bloodlust if they had any plans to leave survivors within striking distance of themselves.

And that is exactly how it has played out. They've intentionally turned Gaza into an uninhabitable wasteland while creating a waking nightmare of death and unfathomable suffering, and Trump and Netanyahu are openly saying that it's not going to end until all the Palestinians have been removed one way or another.

If you're going to rape and torture a child, you probably don't intend to then drop them off at the nearest hospital when you are done with them, because you know the police will be at your door the next day. If you're going to murder your enemy's wife and kids in front of him, you probably don't intend to leave him alive to seek revenge at a later date. Once you've gone all-in on perpetrating a sufficiently terrible act, you often need to do some extra killing on top of it to protect yourself from the consequences of your actions.

That's one of the many reasons why it has always been clear that Israel's intentions for Gaza are genocide and ethnic cleansing. Even if Israeli officials hadn't been making openly genocidal statements, and even if genocidal sentiments hadn't been proliferating throughout the collective consciousness of apartheid Israel for many years — hell, even if you knew absolutely nothing about Israel and Palestine and just looked at the reality on the ground in Gaza — it would still have been obvious to you that Israel did not intend to leave any of those people there. Just because of where they were located and how Israel was treating them.

So when people claim at this late date that they are coming to the reluctant conclusion that Israel is committing genocide in Gaza, I have a hard time believing them. It was obvious to anyone with a basic understanding of human nature that Israel had no intention of leaving any survivors of this mass atrocity on its border. People are just covering their own asses and trying to wash their hands of their guilt for their complicity in a 21st century holocaust over the past 22 months. •

Dare To Hope
• Notes From The Edge Of The Narrative Matrix •

At least 100,000 Australians, including WikiLeaks founder Julian Assange, marched for Gaza across the Sydney Harbour Bridge in the pouring rain at a demonstration on Sunday.

It wasn't that long ago when I sincerely wondered if we'd ever see Assange's face again, let alone in public, let alone in Sydney, let alone heading up what had to be one of the largest pro-Palestine rallies ever held in Australia. Dare to be encouraged. The light is breaking through.

•

The western political/media class is fuming with outrage about images of Israeli hostages who are severely emaciated, which just says so much about how dehumanized Palestinians are in western society. Everyone stop caring about hundreds of thousands of starving Palestinians, it turns out two Israeli hostages are starving in the same way for the same reason.

•

Israel's Foreign Ministry has announced that in order to improve "public diplomacy" efforts the term "hasbara" will no longer be used, because people have come to associate it with lies and propaganda.

The Times of Israel reports:

> "Long referred to as hasbara, a term used to denote both public relations and propaganda that has been freighted with negative baggage in recent years, the ministry now brands its approach as toda'a — which translates to 'awareness' or 'consciousness' — an apparent shift toward broader, more proactive messaging."

That "negative baggage" would of course be public disgust at the nonstop deluge of lies that Israel and its apologists have been spouting for two years to justify an act of genocide. Westerners have grown increasingly aware that Israel and its defenders have a special word for their practice of manipulating public narratives about their beloved apartheid state, so they're changing the word.

Simply stopping the genocide is not considered as an option. Simply ceasing to lie is not considered as an option. They're just changing the word they use for their lies about their genocide.

•

One of the reasons Israel's supporters love to hurl antisemitism accusations at its critics is because it's a claim that can be made without any evidence whatsoever. It's not an accusation based on facts, it's an assertion about someone's private thoughts and feelings, which are invisible. Support for Israel doesn't lend itself to arguments based on facts, logic and morality, so they rely heavily on aggressive claims about what's happening inside other people's heads which cannot be proved or disproved.

It's entirely unfalsifiable. I cannot prove that my opposition to an active genocide is not in fact due to an obsessive hatred of a small Abrahamic religion. I cannot unscrew the top of my head and show everyone that I actually just think it's bad to rain military explosives on top of a giant concentration camp full of children, and am not in fact motivated by a strange medieval urge to persecute Jewish people. So an Israel supporter can freely hurl accusations about what's going on in my head that I am powerless to disprove.

It's been a fairly effective weapon over the years. Campus protests have been stomped out, freedom of expression has been crushed, entire political campaigns have been killed dead, all because it's been normalized to make evidence-free claims about someone's private thoughts and feelings toward Jews if they suggest that Palestinians deserve human rights.

A Harvard professor of Jewish studies named Shaul Magid recently shared the following anecdote:

> "I once asked someone I casually know, an ardent Zionist, 'what could Israel do that would cause you not to support it?'. He was silent for a moment before looking at me and said, 'Nothing.'"

This is horrifying, but facts in evidence indicate that it's also a very common position among Zionists. If you're still supporting Israel at this point, there's probably nothing it could do to lose your support. •

My Letter To Australian MP Mark Dreyfus About Gaza

I wrote the following letter to Mark Dreyfus, my local MP here in Australia:

Dear Mr Dreyfus,

Today I saw the skeleton of a young man in Gaza picked clean by dogs, his arms and head intact but the rest of his body was bone and gristle. The colour of the bones was still a bright fresh red. He had been shot only days ago but the cats and dogs had got to him already and gnawed his bones clean. I have never seen anything like it.

Every single day brings fresh horrors to my screen. Each time I think I can no longer be shocked, I am proven wrong. The image of that man made me gasp. It literally took my breath away. I then had to sit with my hands over my eyes while I waited for my heart and breath to come back to normal.

When I close my eyes at night, all I can see is skeletal babies, their little mouths gaping open like baby birds waiting for a worm. I have started to dream about it. Each night I carry a child, a new child, a different baby, trying to find food for them. I wake up with a shadow of an ache in my arms because in my dreams their bones are as brittle as egg shells and I have to be so tender and careful.

This. Must. Stop. All the waffle of who-did-what-and-when burns to dust when babies are starving. No amount of words can make that right. No amount of words can extinguish the images from my eyes, the ache in my heart, and the alarm going off in my head for those babies.

Please do what you can! I beg of you. Please make it stop. It's all I can think about and I am not alone. Every day the numbers of people like me are growing. Every day more eyes snap awake. •

https://www.caitlinjohnst.one